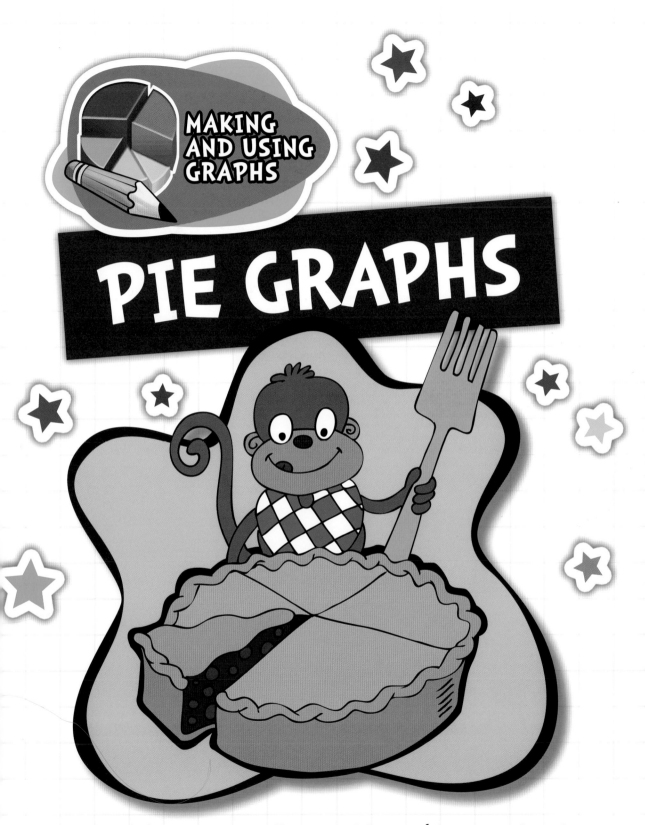

MAKING AND USING GRAPHS

PIE GRAPHS

by Lisa Colozza Cocca   illustrated by Kathleen Petelinsek

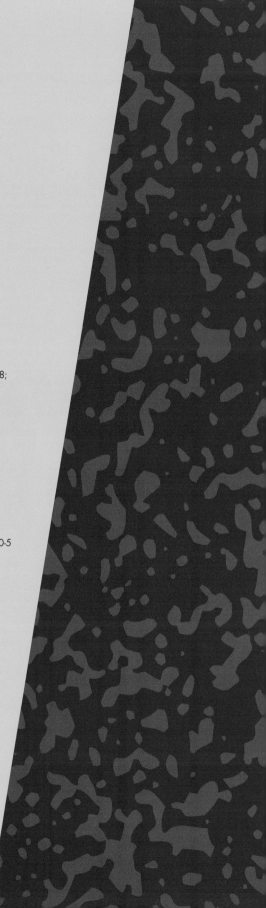

Published in the United States of America by Cherry Lake Publishing
Ann Arbor, Michigan
www.cherrylakepublishing.com

Consultants: Janice Bradley, PhD, Mathematically Connected Communities,
New Mexico State University; Marla Conn, Read-Ability

Editorial direction: Rebecca Rowell
Book design and illustration: The Design Lab

Photo credits: Monkey Business Images/iStockphoto, 4; Shutterstock Images, 8;
iStockphoto, 12; David C. Rehner/Shutterstock Images, 20

Library of Congress Cataloging-in-Publication Data
Cocca, Lisa Colozza, 1957–
  Pie graphs / Lisa Colozza Cocca.
     p. cm. – (Making and using graphs)
  Audience: 005–007
  Audience: Grades K to 3.
  Includes bibliographical references and index.
  ISBN 978-1-61080-915-3 (hardback : alk. paper) – ISBN 978-1-61080-940-5
(paperback : alk. paper) – ISBN 978-1-61080-965-8 (ebook) –
ISBN 978-1-61080-990-0 (hosted ebook)
  1. Mathematics—Graphic methods—Juvenile literature. 2. Fractions—Graphic
methods—Juvenile literature. I. Title.

  QA40.5.C63 2013
  511.5—dc23
                              2012033598

Cherry Lake Publishing would like to acknowledge the work
of The Partnership for 21st Century Skills. Please visit
www.21stcenturyskills.org for more information.

Printed in the United States of America
Corporate Graphics Inc.
January 2013
CLFA10

Table of Contents

CHAPTER ONE

What Is a Pie Graph?

A pie graph can help us compare kids at the park.

Kids. Food. Games. Flowers. These are just a few things we can compare with a pie graph. A pie graph is a type of number picture. A pie graph can help you compare amounts of things.

Some people call a pie graph a circle graph. Do you know why? That's right! A pie graph is shaped like a circle.

Let's learn about pie graphs!

A pie graph has a few parts:

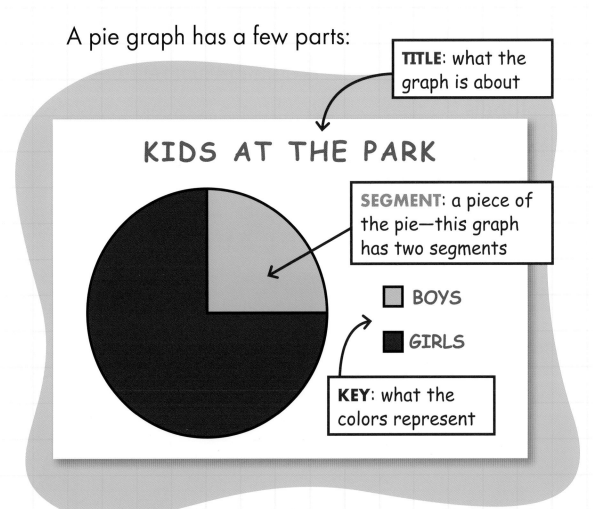

TITLE: what the graph is about

KIDS AT THE PARK

SEGMENT: a piece of the pie—this graph has two segments

☐ BOYS

■ GIRLS

KEY: what the colors represent

This pie graph has data, or information, about kids at the park. The entire circle stands for the whole group. The circle is broken into segments, or parts. The parts are like slices of a pie. Our key, or legend, tells us the green part stands for the boys in the group. The purple part stands for the girls. Were there more boys or girls at the park?

We can make the segments different colors.
That's one reason pie graphs are fun! Let's use
labels this time to show what the segments stand for.

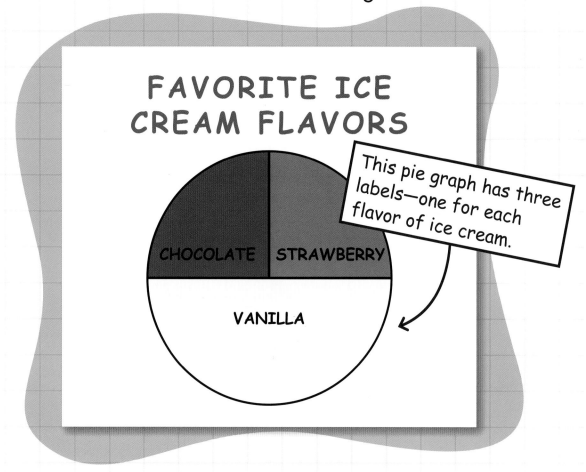

FAVORITE ICE
CREAM FLAVORS

CHOCOLATE | STRAWBERRY

VANILLA

This pie graph has three labels—one for each flavor of ice cream.

The title tells us this pie graph is about our
favorite ice cream flavors. It shows all the flavors
people picked. The labels tell us what each
segment stands for. Which flavor do most
people like best?

Let's compare other things using pie graphs!
Here's what you'll need to complete the activities
in this book:

- notebook paper
- pencil with an eraser
- crayons or markers
- plate or bowl
- ruler

Gather what you need.

CHAPTER TWO

Graphing Pizza

A pizza is like a pie graph! It's round and cut into segments.

Let's get some pizza! We need to know what toppings people want. There are so many choices. We can use a pie graph to show our data. We'll use the pie graph to help us order the right toppings.

Our pizza pie graph is divided, or cut, into three parts. Each part is a different color. Each part stands for something we can put on our pizza.

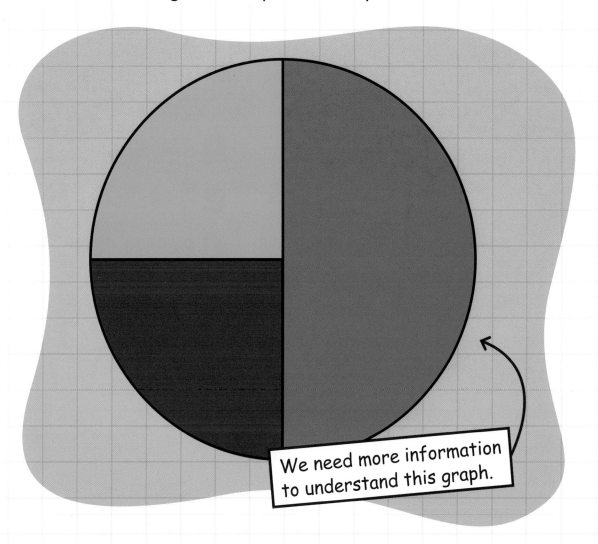

We need more information to understand this graph.

Oh no! We can't read the pie graph. What's missing?

What do we need to understand the pie graph? That's right! We need labels or a key.

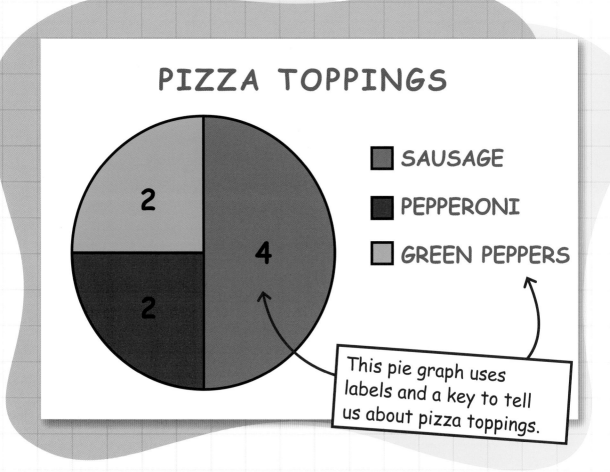

PIZZA TOPPINGS

■ SAUSAGE

■ PEPPERONI

□ GREEN PEPPERS

This pie graph uses labels and a key to tell us about pizza toppings.

We can read the graph now. It has labels and a key. Two people want pepperoni on the pizza. How many people want green peppers? Which topping do most people want?

Add Labels

Practice adding labels to a pie graph.

INSTRUCTIONS:

1. Draw the pie graph from page 9 onto paper. To make a circle, you can trace around a plate or bowl. Ask an adult for help getting a dish. If you want, use your ruler to make the lines to cut the circle into pieces.
2. Color in the parts of the graph.
3. Add labels to tell what the parts stand for.
4. Write the title above the graph.

To get a copy of this activity, visit www.cherrylakepublishing.com/activities.

Pizza Toppings

CHAPTER THREE

Graphing Playground Fun

Let's use a pie graph to show what kids like to do at the playground.

Playing at a park is fun. We can swing, slide, play on the monkey bars, and more.

The playground is busy. Lots of kids are here. Let's make a pie graph to show what they like to do at the playground.

A tally chart can help us track how many children like each activity best. To tally is to count. We can use the chart to record what we count. We make a **tally mark**, or line, for each thing we count. The fifth mark goes across the other four.

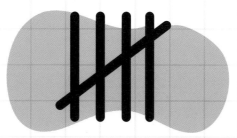

Next, we count the tally marks in each row. We write the numbers in the chart.

PLAYGROUND FUN		
ACTIVITY	NUMBER OF KIDS	TOTAL
Slide	||	2
Swings	|||||		6
Monkey Bars	||||	4

A tally chart is a great way to record the data we need to create a pie graph.

We can use our data to make a pie graph. The whole circle stands for all of the children's choices. It's divided into three segments. We add labels this time.

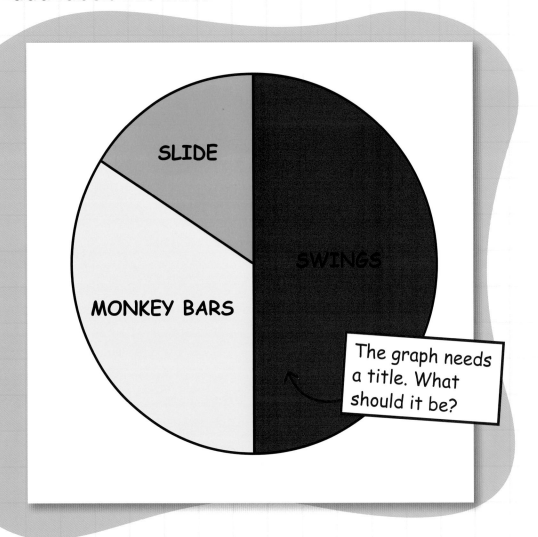

What would be a good title for our pie graph? Which activity was most popular?

Add a Key

Practice adding a key to a pie graph.

INSTRUCTIONS:

1. Copy the pie graph from page 14 onto paper. If you want, use a round dish and your ruler to make the graph. Don't add the labels!
2. Write a title above the graph.
3. Make a key to show what the parts stand for.

To get a copy of this activity, visit www.cherrylakepublishing.com/activities.

CHAPTER FOUR

Graphing Flowers

Let's graph flower colors!

Look at our pretty flowers! We have four different colors. We can make a pie graph to compare how many flowers of each color we have.

We start by sorting the flowers by color. We have eight flowers. We cut our circle into eight equal parts, like slicing a pie into eight pieces.

We color in one part for each flower. First, we color four parts pink for the four pink flowers.

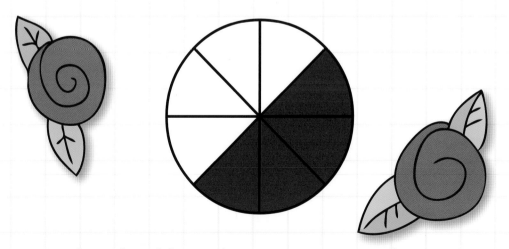

What should we do next? You're right. We need to color the other four parts.

We color the other parts. We add a title and a key, too. Here's our finished pie chart.

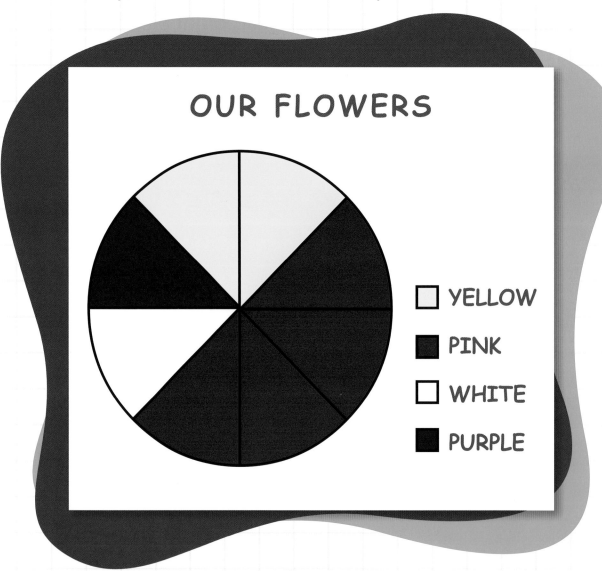

OUR FLOWERS

☐ YELLOW

■ PINK

☐ WHITE

■ PURPLE

How many different colored parts do we have? Which color flower do we have the most of?

To get a copy of this activity, visit www.cherrylakepublishing.com/activities.

ACTIVITY

Graph Coins

Practice making a pie graph about money.

INSTRUCTIONS:
1. Copy the pie graph from the top of page 17 onto your paper. If you want, use a round dish and your ruler to make the graph. Don't add any color yet!
2. Put some pennies, nickels, dimes, and quarters in a bag.
3. Without looking, pull eight coins out of the bag.
4. Sort the eight coins into four groups: pennies, nickels, dimes, and quarters. Focus only on the different sizes of the coins. Don't think about amounts.
5. Color the parts of your pie graph to show the groups. Remember to put all of the penny parts next to each other. Do the same with the other coins.
6. Add labels or a key.
7. Give your pie graph a title.
8. Share your pie graph with a friend. Can he or she tell which type of coin you pulled most often?

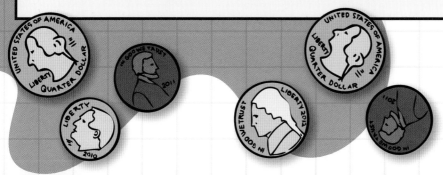

CHAPTER FIVE

Pie Graphs Are Fun

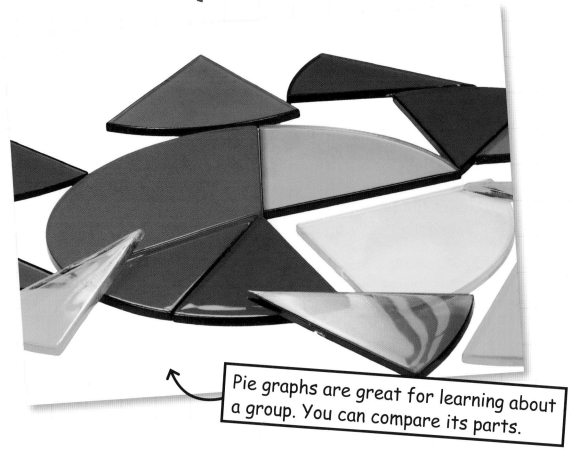

Pie graphs are great for learning about a group. You can compare its parts.

Pie graphs are fun to make and easy to read. They can help us compare the parts of a whole group. They can show us what we have the most of and the least of. Or they can tell us what is most popular or least popular.

What is your favorite thing to show in a pie graph? Start looking and find out!

What else can you show in a pie graph? Here are some ideas:

- Compare types of two-legged animals and four-legged animals at the zoo.
- Study the different colors of towels in a laundry basket or closet.
- Figure out which color backpack is most popular in your class.
- Find out which game or sport you and your friends like to play most.

With a pie graph, you can compare animals at the zoo.

Glossary

data (DAY-tuh) information recorded about people or things

key (kee) a list or chart that tells what the pictures or symbols in a graph stand for; also called a legend

label (LAY-buhl) a name

record (ri-KORD) to write down

row (roh) a line of data that goes from side to side

segment (SEG-muhnt) a part or piece of something

tally chart (TAL-ee chahrt) a way to record things you count that uses tally marks

tally mark (TAL-ee mahrk) a line that stands for one item of something being counted

title (TYE-tuhl) the name of a chart

For More Information

BOOKS

Bieder, Bonnie. *Graphs*. New York: Grosset & Dunlap, 2003.

Bodach, Vijaya Khisty. *Pie Graphs: Making Graphs*. Mankato, MN: Capstone, 2008.

Decastro, Amy. *Sort, Graph, & Tally*. Westminster, CA: Teacher Created Resources, 2003.

WEB SITES

Math Playground—Circle Graphs and Pie Charts
www.mathplayground.com/piechart.html
Add labels and data to make your own pie graph.

Kids' Zone: Learning with NCES—Create a Graph
nces.ed.gov/nceskids/createagraph/
Make a pie graph with this online tutorial.

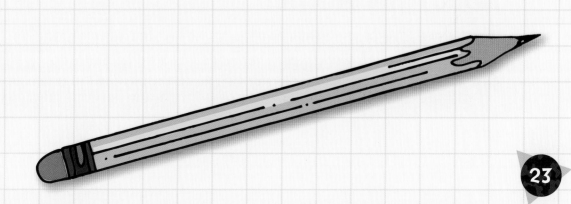

Index

About the Author

Lisa Colozza Cocca is a former teacher and school librarian. For the past decade, she has worked as a freelance writer and editor. She lives, works, and plays in New Jersey. Lisa thinks graphs are lots of fun.